Yoga In A

Business Suit

Everything I Learned About Business,

I Learned In Yoga

Ken Grant

MBPRESS

Yoga In A Business Suit

Everything I Learned About Business, I Learned In Yoga

MotivatedBrandingPress (MBPress)

(MBPress is a division of MotivatedBranding)

P.O.Box 1315

Edmonds, WA 98020

MotivatedBranding.com

MotivatedBrandingPress

ISBN - 13: 978-0615972718
ISBN - 10: 0615972713
LCCN: 2014903818

10 9 8 7 6 5 4 3 2 1

SPECIAL SALES
MBPress books are available at special discounts for bulk purchases for sales promotions and gifts. Special editions including personalized covers can be developed in large quantities for special corporate/association needs. For more information, please email: info@motivatedbranding.com

ACKNOWLEDGMENTS

My darling, über-supportive wife, Kristin

To the original A & Z: my daughters Annalisa and Zoë

To Pat Coussens for believing and pushing

In memory of my Mum, Laurel Grant 1935-2013

My remarkable Dad, Doug Grant - my true hero

Editing Team: Matt Fontaine, Teri Citterman and Geri Skelly

Acarya: Cheryl Fernandez

Cover: Rhombus, Inc.

Cover photography: Michael Craft Photography

DEDICATION

There is not a day that goes by when I am not inspired by my friends, family and God.

In return, this amazing combination of super heroes allows me to be bold, persistent and passionate for the art and science of branding.

This books is dedicated to all the dreamers in the world, and converting their dreams into reality.

CONTENTS

10 Key Principles

HISTORY

Did you know that close to 15 million Americans practice the art of yoga every year? And that 70,000+ people are involved as yoga instructors? Or that it is a $10B+ industry? Who knew that yoga, that crazy exercise that pushes, twists and cajoles your body into places where you did not know you could move to, would be so popular!

If you saw me, you would agree I do not look like anything remotely close to a yoga fan – maybe more like a yogurt fan. But, I practice Ashtanga Vinyasa Yoga every Wednesday and I swear that it quite literally is saving my life on a weekly basis. I love yoga because it slows me down for a moment; it allows me to proverbially 'catch my breath' and it reconnects me with my center.

If you are anything like me – business owner, family man, a person always on the go, go, go – I can hang on pretty tight at times. Yoga wrings that tension out of me, forcing me to do something that is not within my normal comfort zone. Yet, in retrospect, yoga probably provides me with just what my human body inherently and naturally needs – a need that isn't completely met by running a business, having a family and being part of the oh-too-common rat race!

Every Wednesday evening I show up at the gym and make my way to the quiet solitude of the yoga room. Here, I unfurl my yoga mat and wait for instruction from my intrepid trainer, my Acarya, Cheryl. There I am, doing my Virabhadrasana II and Downward Facing Dogs accompanied by the low hum of a soundtrack built for Buddha – breathing out the stress of life and breathing in a new lease on life.

On one of these yoga-filled evenings, I was doing my thing like everyone else in our tranquil room. I was breathing, stretching and otherwise being a good student, when I started to hear words coming out of my instructor's mouth that struck me like a ton of bricks. Have you ever been that one person in a situation who sees or hears things so differently than everyone else around you? That was me in class that evening.

Cheryl would talk about finding and strengthening our core, and all I could hear was how pertinent that was in my world of branding and solid company business practices. *A brand without a core is not a brand at all!* Then she talked about inner strength and that I am the <u>only</u> one who can push me as far as I can go – no one else can do it for me. *It is only when I bring myself to the very edge that I will truly learn.* Again, WOW! I would so often think to myself, "Am I the only person in the room who is hearing this?" And that was just the beginning.

Week after week, my mind was swimming with these yoga words, instructions and poses that so perfectly correlated into professional and personal branding and business leadership. At the end of every class, I would dash out and run to the club's front desk, asking for pen and paper. My mind was exploding as I discovered more and more of these powerful similarities to business and branding. These resemblances grew and grew and the notes piled higher and higher on my office desk. Those notes were what birthed this book, and in turn became the penultimate 'Chapter Y' in the larger encyclopedic book: *The A-to-Z of Brand Rejuvenation* (released through MotivatedBrandingPress in 2014).

How amazing were these words flying around the yoga studio! They were filled with so many strong metaphors and unbelievably pertinent parallels between the art of yoga and the hard-hitting edges of business. More specifically, they were a guide for how to grow, to expand, to live life to the fullest and never be afraid to take bold action for yourself and those around you.

Who knew that yoga, that crazy exercise that pushes, twists and cajoles your body into positions where you never knew you could go, would also lead to the opening of a special door! A door through which we can learn so much about our own personal brands, and the brands we manage and work for every day.

Even if you have never had the chance to take a yoga class in your life, I promise that the metaphors, parallels and symbolism will still make a great deal of sense to you.

So here is to your success and ever-evolving growth — to living a life where you feel in charge of you and your own self-worth. Where you uncover things about your own inherent power what will push you to new and exciting heights and leave the old you in the rear view mirror. Here is to you, appreciating that it truly takes a village to move mountains, while balancing the need for self-reflection and the importance of slowing down and taking it all in. Here is to you being <u>you</u>!

Please   enjoy   *Yoga   In   A   Business   Suit.*

Ken Grant

Principle 1:

Everything is centered to our core

If that doesn't sound like the perfect brand, I don't know what does. Everything we do and touch with our brand, all centers back to its core.

A brand is not simply about its extensions, its outward face, its happy face, i.e., marketing. That is just part of it. Everything to do with your brand, just like we as humans, is centered to and around a main nucleus: our heart, our soul, our center, our core. A brand without a heart is nothing I want anything to do with and come to find out, neither do most customers. And given the short life expectancy of many brands, the ones without a strong core have a greater chance of simply falling to pieces.

Yoga also demonstrates to us that exposing your core is not a bad thing. At first you feel completely naked and vulnerable. Just like brands, we as people have been hardwired over the years to protect our souls, our hearts and our center for fear that someone will not like us, turn away, and never come back.

If we have learned anything about small to mid-sized companies over the past decade or so, it is that our audience likes it when we are real and yes, vulnerable. And as in business, personal branding is all about that, too. We want authentic – not fake – and the only way to get that is to be OK with who we are on the inside. To truly comprehend and recognize what is at our core.

In business there is so much that hinges on the core of your brand. Its entire positioning, the culture, your employee branding, the way you hire and train, the products you produce and the services you provide –

everything stems from the core. And without a tight core, things have nothing to connect to and fall apart.

Ken Grant

Principle 2:

Pushing, Extending and

Expanding yourself

Yoga is all about pushing yourself. Extending your mind and body to places you didn't know you could go and expanding beyond what you thought possible – beyond one's comfort zone!

But at the same time, you cannot go beyond your own self. That is the whole point of yoga – to push, to expand, to learn and to grow. It is to make it about ourselves, not the competition.

Our bodies and brands are so similar. We should never be OK with the status quo, with just getting away with things or sitting back and putting it on autopilot. We need to expand, push, lengthen and stretch ourselves (our brands).

Yoga for your business is no different. By pushing your own limits, you get to know yourself so much better. The best part is that you can only push yourself as far as you can physically go. I cannot do things that you can do and you cannot do things that I can do. I can only push myself as far as my own limits will take me. It is brilliant if you think about it. That means you have to be completely, 100% honest with yourself. You must discover your own limits, your own strengths, your *own* self. This means you are being true to yourself, just as you would your brand. It is within this self-reflection that you get a glimpse of what you are completely capable of.

Brands are no different – you just need to always be pushing the boundaries of what your brand is totally capable of, not simply being satisfied with what you can get away with.

Principle 3:

Focus is everything

If there is one thing yoga teaches us, it is how to focus. Ideally, while you are in your yoga practice nothing else should be distracting your mind or body. Otherwise you may as well not be there. It is this focus that allows us to find our inner strength and guides us safely to our own limits.

This intense focus can be duplicated in the business world. Since you cannot be all things to all people, you must determine what it is that you are so good at –

that *one thing* no else can touch. In other words, it is more about depth than breadth – discovering your own unique sales proposition and brands positioning in the marketplace.

So many companies and people I meet firmly believe that they and/or their company can be all things to all people. That just can't be true. Outside of things like water and food, I cannot put my finger on a solitary product or service on the planet today that has that power. Heck, even with food and water we have choices these days.

However, I empathize with this notion about being all things to all people. It is not always easy to focus, but the more you become great at something, the more people around you will also appreciate that *thing*, that expertise.

We are reluctant to focus on only one thing. It is scary to have *all our eggs in one basket*! We get petrified that without having a hundred options to sell, we're nothing. But this is the era of specialization. I contend that instead of having one hundred different doors with potentially one person behind each door (all of which takes time and energy to reach), that we focus on just *one* door. That one door could potentially have one hundred like-minded people behind it, all of them waiting to play and interact with us.

Knocking on a hundred doors, instead of just one, invites instant exhaustion. And yes, people might think that putting the focus on only one door might get boring over time. But again, I contend that you will just get better at that one thing, honing your skills until you know you have exhausted all possibilities. Then you know it truly is time to evolve into something else.

Another way of thinking about this is the concept of knowing a little about a lot or knowing a lot about a little. Although the former sounds exciting and can be to your advantage at a cocktail party, knowing more on certain subjects makes you an expert. I know these are two extreme examples, but I do not want my plumber doing my taxes or my car detailer being my heart surgeon.

Permit yourself, your company and your staff to be experts at something and watch what happens to your market positioning and indeed your revenue when you do. You will be amazed how possessing a specific skill or talent can captivate your audience.

Principle 4:

Being Present = Being Relevant

As in business, yoga doesn't work if you are not fully present. It is difficult to 'dial-in' yoga. Being present is all about 'being in the now'. Being in the now is about being real, which is about being honest, and caring for your personal (and professional) brand, your people, your brand experience and your customer experience. In other words, it is all about truly 'Showing-Up'.

Being present keeps things relevant and fresh, never left behind and forgotten. Being fully aware means you appreciate yesterday, what you will be doing today, and how to look forward to an improved tomorrow. It means letting go of the garbage and only caring about the stuff that matters. In the 'right now' is really all we can ever worry about anyway, right?!

Our challenge in modern times is not letting our busy lives overtake us. Too much technology, crazy deadlines, social media obsessions, doing too much in any given hour, never finishing something, or if you are anything like me, having the 'shiny ball syndrome' can be exhausting. We can be bombarded with so much extrasensory nonsense – the test is slowing all that down so we can get stuff done. *Quality vs. quantity!*

Rest your mind as we do on the yoga mat – if only for twenty minutes a day – find your center and start thinking through what is necessary to get done and what is extraneous. By prioritizing, things will become clear as to what needs to get done first. Sadly, in my mind it always looks like I am carrying too many bags through a small door – forcing too much to happen all at once.

The second we do not force things is the moment we can be present to the things around us that are of the most importance: family, friends, health, and well-being. Or if you think of this in business terms, it is taking better care of ourselves, our staff and our customers. Being present allows those around you to see that you really do care; that you are working, thinking and being in the 'now'; that you are putting aside the visible and invisible distractions.

Being present also means you appreciate today and what today is worth to you. Too many companies (and people) hang on so tightly to yesterday. It's like they truly believe it was a better era. To what end? The past is just that − if you have filled your past with great moments and memories, then go ahead and cherish that, but there is no need to drag all that forward with you. If you have lived a life of purpose, then your past can rest easily back in the past. It is only in the now, that we can truly appreciate what we have today.

When we are present, we can be relevant. And in today's business environment, if you are not relevant, you have a higher chance of not making it into tomorrow. Being relevant includes being present to today's trends, people's likes and dislikes. Being relevant is evolving with the times with your products, services, sales and marketing vehicles, as well as providing the best customer experience possible.

Presence and relevance are about being alive, about energy and passion for what you are doing now. In this fast paced world, being relevant rules the day. As I recently said to one iconic client (a famed restaurant, 60 years in business), as a customer, we care more about the next 60 seconds and how you treat us, than the past 60 years you have been in business – be as relevant as you can be. Be bold moving forward and leave the past in the past. You will be glad you did, as tomorrow will reward you for your boldness, evolution and forward thinking.

Principle 5:

Open communication

Have you ever noticed that the yoga instructor (or any coach for that matter) is always leading you through what is happening? You are rarely left to your own devices. You are when it comes to doing a pose or an exercise, but great instructors walk you through everything. You are never left wondering why you are doing something, or how that one pose connects to the next. In general, great sports coaches are quite similar – always chattering away, encouraging, teaching and keeping everyone apprised of the direction the team is headed; they are always explaining why you are doing what is asked of you.

Take this personally. Communicating your vision to everyone on your team so they appreciate the big picture and the direction you are taking them as their leader is critical to reaching greater success.

Ever seen how a great professional kitchen works? There is always chatter, a buzz, a sense of great camaraderie. This stems from the head chef, pushing, chatting and otherwise keeping everyone and everything moving in a coherent direction. It is all done through powerful communications.

Or, think of a great maestro in front of his orchestra and his ease and ability to communicate his art form through the use of his baton. The baton extends the conductor's voice to their team. With a simple twitch, swipe or flurry, he or she sends specific directions to parts or all of the orchestra. Again – open and frequent communication is key.

Be the yoga instructor at your company. Be in tune with your people, helping articulate what is happening every step of the way. This doesn't have to be done at the same rate as the yoga instructor, or the chef, or the conductor. And it need not be in a torrential way with too much information coming at your employees in a huge downpour. Simply lead and articulate by example. This way, your people will appreciate and understand that you are all in this together, and yet reinforces that you are ultimately their leader.

Think of the three C's of Communication: Concise, Consistent and Constant.

Ken Grant

Principle 6:

You are not alone

You may be noticing an underlying theme. We are pushing, growing and evolving. We are focused, we are chatting and we know what is at our core. However, look around the room. You will quickly realize you are also never alone. Who knew that yoga could be considered a team sport?

Many business owners, whom I have met, often share a similar story or challenge. They tell me, "I feel so isolated." Or, "It is lonely at the top." However, if you change your mindset about who is actually around you, you will start to see that you are not as isolated as you might think.

If you follow best practices around hiring, training and vision (see *The A-to-Z of Brand Rejuvenation*) you will automatically be surrounded by people who are more in step with you than ever before. Trust these people to help support and communicate what is going on around your brand, your company.

Unless you have the attitude that it is me vs. them, you should be soliciting and empowering your team to see the future *with* you. When you do, you should never feel alone. Yes, it comes down to *you* and how *you* conduct yourself as a leader at work. But like yoga, you are surrounded by people who are also trying to do better. Try shifting your perspective and you will feel less isolated.

There is fun twist to 'not being alone.' Studies continue to highlight that the #2 reason people stay at their job is because of the friends they make while at work. *Community*. This is a huge deal, even in the smallest of companies. This is the perfect reason to hire People-People into your culture. Your staff wants to feel comfortable at work and have people around them who they can trust.

Do this correctly, and your people should also never feel like they are stranded on an island with no one around to befriend them.

Principle 7:

No Pain = No Gain

I have heard my instructor say on more than one occasion (try hundreds of times) that doing something for one minute never killed anyone. Yes, there are some situations in life where everything can change in the blink of an eye. But for this conversation, I think you get what I'm saying – pushing hard and outside your comfort zone generally won't kill you – it just makes you stronger.

In checking the morning obituary page, it is uncommon to read, "James O'Brien died from pushing too hard and trying to better his life!" So if you can't die from doing it, why are so many people opposed to taking on change? Not taking on change for change sake, but in order to fix a problem or to simply evolve.

Ask any physical trainer and they will reaffirm the fact that "no pain = no gain!" It is also true in business. If you are having any problems with your brand today, I wonder which is more painful? Sticking with what you are doing and expecting circumstances to change (the true meaning of insanity)? *The status quo.* Or doing the work it takes to make a true and sustainable difference in your future? *Ever advancing your brand.* Sometimes change can hurt. But it is worth it in the long run, otherwise we are back to not being relevant.

Here is an interesting twist on the No Pain = No Gain principle. Many companies are rife with a cancerous disease. Call it: poor employees, bad investors, or incongruous inventory ... whatever! If this is the case, it is time to operate and cut the cancer out. If it were in your body, you probably would not hesitate to get it out TODAY!!!! So why hold your company to a different standard? Yes it will hurt. *Pain.* But it will hurt less than letting things fester and get worse. *Gain.*

Yoga is no different. Once you get into the mindset that what you are doing might hurt a little, but you realize you are doing it for the betterment of you, then the pain is most certainly worth it. The pain is short lived while the benefits are long lasting.

I suggest small, frequent tweaks to your brand (like working out) instead of waiting until things get so bad that your ability to change the future looks like it will be too painful to go through. One goes to yoga every week to see gradual, sustainable change, not once a year to see a miraculous change which we all know does not exist!

Principle 8:

Compassion

If Yoga teaches us one thing, it is the fact that it is OK for you to have compassion for yourself. In yoga, we also learn that it is good to have compassion for those around us – which, depending on who you are, might be a struggle.

Having compassion for those around us seems to be a 'silly' and outdated business notion in a world that is all about crushing the competition. But having compassion is coming back into style.

Imagine you are not nice to your employees, your

peers or your business partners, but the second a customer walks through the door, you become a different person, bending over backwards to meet their every whim. I'd call that a true Jekyll and Hyde situation, wouldn't you? You've seen it; I've seen it. And maybe reading this, you know I'm talking about you. Come on! Compassion is something we must have for *everyone* around us, not just the ones we know need to see it in order to make a sale!

Yoga informs us that it is OK to let down your guard. And it is perfectly OK to be human. In this day and age, that is downright refreshing and will open up a level of empathy for you and those around you. That alone will blow your competitors out of the water.

Think of compassion as karma – what goes around, comes around. Compassion for others is refreshing – it is compelling – it is transformational. And it is the way of the future, so get used to it, because it ain't going away!

Principle 9:

Flexibility

If there is one thing we all know about yoga, it is the fact that everything is about flexibility. That is the guiding principle. The more we move, the more we flex and the more we flex, presumably the healthier we get. I have friends that are physical therapists and when they train with senior adults, they swear by the same thing: if they could convince their clients to do only one simple exercise each and every day, it would be stretch and flex.

Similarly, if there is one thing about business we can all appreciate, it is to always expect the unexpected. This is clearly easier to do when you are flexible. You need to practice flexibility with yourself as a business owner, with your staff and their happiness, with your expectations around work culture, and ultimately, the needs of your customers, guests and clients.

This is no longer a rigid world that we live in. Things can quite literally change overnight. We are only as good as our reputation is today. So knowing this, we need to roll with the punches, thinking ahead of our own game, watching for sustainable trends and being OK with change. *Really OK!*

If stretching and flexing is good for our physical bodies, then it has to be good for our businesses, too. So every morning as you get ready for your day, breathe in and out, slowly and purposefully thinking about the twists and turns you may face today. I'm not saying confront, but face. And know that your ability to be flexible with people and situations will probably drive you to your biggest wins and successes at the end of the day.

The more flexible you are in the toughest situations, means you will be more capable of finding solutions – not hanging on for dear life, hoping this, too, will blow over.

You also don't always have to be right, which allows you to move on with life without the extra baggage or harboring ill will.

Ken Grant

Principle 10:

Time for Reflection = Balance

As much as I am quoted about recommending people be completely, 100% obsessed about what you do and for doing it well, there is something to be said about taking a breather. Even if it is just for a moment from time to time, be sure to take a minute just for yourself and by yourself. *Some alone time.*

As our lives become more unbalanced, yoga teaches us that balance in our life is critical to our own happiness and wellbeing.

If we don't have balance and time for reflection in our

lives, we start to lose sight of what is important. We hang on too tightly and that can lead to bad things over time, including a lack of clarity and/or perspective in our lives.

It is not surprising to see a strong connection between the average age of company leaders these days and the average age of a yoga attendee. 45-64. This is the segment of our community with increased stress in their life, being pulled in a million different directions and the ones seeking greater work-life balance. During this period of our lives, it seems a very natural time to re-discover greater clarity for what we want moving forward. This pertains to us personally and professionally.

Maybe we are fighting the urge to hang on to 'stuff' too tightly. Or maybe we are scared we are losing focus on those around us and our compassion for others. Or maybe we are becoming scattered and less focused. It is no different in business, because businesses are simply a manifestation of the people who own and run them. The business leader who is hanging on too tightly, scared of his/her own shadow vs. taking the time needed to reflect on the problem(s) at hand affects every person in the workplace. *Being present.*

I believe it is OK to let your staff know that you will be unplugging for a short while in order to find the time to unwind – for your own sake and for the sake of those around you. Take a spa day, take yourself to the beach, hit the gym or the links or simply have a glass of wine at that bar across town you have been meaning to go to.

The greatest pleasure yoga brings us is the ability to find a little alone time. *In my case, my alone time is every Wednesday evening.* During this time I get the go-ahead to 'spoil' myself – and if only for an hour – it gives me the chance to recharge my batteries.

This is permission-based, so grant yourself the permission it takes to take time off and do it guilt free! Your mind and body will thank you for it. Your loved ones will thank you for it. The universe will thank you for it.

Ken Grant

Shavasana

Time to take it all in

At the end of the day, appreciate the fact that YOU are totally worth the work you have put into this. You have made an investment in yourself by stretching and connecting to your core – learning to be flexible. And by offering true compassion to yourself and others, everyone benefits: your company, staff, customers, your friends and family, and most importantly you. Every single one of the people that can help you to make your vision happen are all worth it, too.

People have high expectations of you. They look up to you. They regard you with great worthiness and maybe even aspire to be you; so the more you 'Show-Up', the more you bring your entire self to the world. We often underestimate all the talents we do bring to the table, or we only bring the bits and pieces we believe people will want to see, so bring it all. And let those around you be inspired by whatever part of you *they* want to connect with and share with you.

Be OK being you: flaws, imperfections, egos, challenges – the lot. Forever grow and evolve – live your life the way you want to live it, not vicariously through someone else. Don't be told what to do – tell yourself what to do! It is your life and the only one you get, so make it count.

Namaste

Top 10 Yoga/Business moves

1. In business, as in yoga, everything is centered around our **core**. Without this, our brand (personal or professional) has nothing to root to. Our core brings forth our authentic self – and represents our unshakable values.

2. Apart from some rare exceptions, in general no one dies from **Pushing, Extending and Expanding**. Rarely have we ever seen a business shut down because of trying and discovering its peak performance. It is all about discovering how far you can go, within your own skin. Only at the edge, can we grow.

3. Focus is everything in yoga, as it is in business, and in life. Without focus, we think we can be all things to all people. This is a difficult stunt to pull off. So be really good at what YOU are good at, because people love an expert.

4. Being Present is the name of the game in life. Without being present, we do not honor ourselves or the person sitting across from us with 'all' that we can be. *Truly 'Showing-Up'*. In brands, when we are present we are relevant.

5. Open **communication** is a must in modern business. We not only want to know why we are rowing in the same direction, but which direction we are expected to row. And like great chefs, the more chatter in the kitchen, the better the outcome on the table. *Concise, Consistent, Constant Communication.*

6. Never think for a moment that you are **alone** in business. Like Yoga, business is not a solitary sport; it is a team sport. If you have your head turned toward the corner feeling sorry that you are all alone at the top, put real players around you that will support you and help you (and them) grow and flourish.

7. No one ever went to the gym and expected miraculous changes after being there an hour. Consider it this way; think of your brand challenges or mishaps as weight gain – the extra weight we put on did not happen overnight, so losing weight won't happen overnight either. **No Pain = No Gain**. Be OK with the fact that what you are accomplishing through brand rejuvenation is no walk in the park and not for the faint hearted. But, you can do this; the little bit of pain to do the work will be worth the journey back to good business health and a more rewarding brand.

8. Compassion is the only way to play in business today. What does the absence of compassion leave you with? If you do not use compassion, then how else would you treat your people, your customers or even yourself? Successful, modern brands are all about transparency and a willingness to share of themselves – this starts with compassion for yourself and the capacity to be real.

9. Flexibility, like compassion, can go a long way. As in yoga, the more flexible you are, the less chance you have of straining something. In modern day business, if you are hanging on too tightly, things can and will break. We need to be flexible with everything we touch, because it can and will change quickly.

10. When was the last time you took time off to either recharge your batteries or simply **reflect** on what you have accomplished? If the answer is either "infrequently" or "I do not recall" then it is time to take a break. Take a break for the good of you and those around you. Take it from me – yoga saves my life on a weekly basis. Just the chance to unwind and not think about anything but my breathing, energizes me back to the level I need to completely 'Show-Up'. Try it – your business will still be there when you get back.

Author Bio

Life for Australian born, Ken Grant started in the spotlight. As a classically trained musician – violinist, pianist and composer – Ken's early success includes claiming the title of youngest lead second violinist in the history of the Melbourne Philharmonic.

Further success lead him to Northern California where he wrote a children's musical and released his first CD, California Outback. In addition to music, Ken hosted his own TV Public Affairs show and worked as a sought after radio DJ.

Ken moved to Seattle in 1995 and changed his focus from music to marketing and immediately entrenched himself into brand development. Finding success in building brands such as the mega-Australian wine brand: *Alice White*, Ken found his true passion was in resuscitating brands that were exhausted and worn-out. As a partner and Brand Strategist for a Seattle ad agency, Ken rebranded a myriad of companies within various sectors including: Retail, Destination/Tourism, Food & Beverage, Banking and Non Profit.

At the helm of MotivatedBranding, Ken continues to build his reputation for turning companies around – starting from the inside out. Being a firm believer that companies should not change the exterior touch points of the brand until strong modifications have been made on the inside, Ken's relentless style has paid off more times than not. No matter the format, from public speaking to writing, breakouts, broadcast and advising, the takeaway is commanding: Break away from the commoditization and learn 'The

Art of Differentiation'.

It is Ken's tenacious spirit and love for branding that led to the development and publishing of *The A-to-Z of Brand Rejuvenation* and *Yoga In A Business Suit* - and the BiteSize BigIdea[tm] book series. Integrated with his books are: keynotes and workshops, a publishing division (MBPress), newsletters, an educational division with online learning modules and a learning reference app, (MBU), a full social compliment including: Facebook, Twitter and YouTube channel, and interactive testing documents to help owners of companies turn their branded worlds around for good.

Ken is a family man – wife and two daughters. He resides in the Puget Sound waterfront town of Edmonds (a Seattle, Washington suburb.)

Ken's passions include: photography, piano, wine, yoga, automobiles, sailing, biking, triathlons, cooking, travel and electronica music.

MB**PRESS**

39912058R00036

Made in the USA
Charleston, SC
22 March 2015